Boa Editions
INDEPENDENT PUBLISHING SINCE 1976

Sidekick

Sidekick

Naomi Shihab Nye

AMERICAN POETS CONTINUUM SERIES NO. 223
BOA EDITIONS ✢ ROCHESTER, NY ✢ 2026

First Edition
23 24 25 26 7 6 5 4 3 2 1

Publications by Boa Editions—a nonprofit corporation under section 501 (c) (3) of the United States Internal Revenue Code—are made possible with funds from a variety of sources, including public funds from the Literature Program of the National Endowment for the Arts; the New York State Council on the Arts, a state agency; and the County of Monroe, NY. Private funding sources include the Max and Marian Farash Charitable Foundation; the Mary S. Mulligan Charitable Trust; the Rochester Area Community Foundation; the Ames Amzalak Memorial Trust in memory of Henry Ames, Semon Amzalak, and Dan Amzalak; and contributions from many individuals nationwide. See Colophon on page 175 for special individual acknowledgments.

Cover Design: Sandy Knight
Cover Art: "Two Siberian Boys" by Michael Nye, 1992
Interior Design and Composition: Isabella Madeira
Boa Logo: Sandy Knight

Boa Editions books are available electronically through BookShare, an online distributor offering Large-Print, Braille, Multimedia Audio Book, and Dyslexic formats, as well as through e-readers that feature text to speech capabilities.

Cataloging-in-Publication Data is available from the Library of Congress.

State of the Arts
NYSCA

Boa Editions
250 North Goodman Street, Suite 306
Rochester, NY 14607
www.boaeditions.org
A. Poulin, Jr., Founder (1938-1996)

For Mikey—
I'm your sidekick all the way.

"I arise in the morning torn between a desire to improve (or save) the world and a desire to enjoy (or savor) the world. This makes it hard to plan the day."

—E.B. White

"Stay vigilant in this slender moment."

—Sean Sexton

Contents

2 *"We need our petit absorptions like campstools in the wilderness"*
—Jack Kerouac

Ambition

I've been at a poetry reading all my life.
Whispering pine trees, now bamboo,
subtle green undercurrents, how could anyone
not hear them?

Syllables along green river,
in line at grocery, poems floating our ways,
every month laden, every troubled,
layered, curious day.

What is your ambition?
caused me to plummet.
Peering for clues wherever I went.
To scrawl. Absorb it all.

To be aware, as Gary Snyder
said, of every single one-time-only
moment. Not to miss it. In 1930,
Ghandi wrote, *Be truthful, gentle, fearless.*

Might that be ambition?

My personal position is clear.

I hate all war.

This is what we were living for.

To find a personal position on a planet,

on a page. Visiting Ghandi's Delhi home,

I found his bed so low and white—

a child might easily sleep there.

1

Raiment of Birdsong, Believe in Us As We Stagger On

Anthem of the Sidekick

How are my people?

Who are my people?

Where are my people?

How many people

can anyone have?

Did anyone sleep?

How could they sleep?

Did soldiers weep?

Why did they weep?

Why did they not weep?

What is this netherworld?

Is this a haven?

Aren't we lucky to be here?

What did we forget?

How was it forgotten?

Did anyone pray before killing?

How could they pray?

Where were the windows?

Where were the doors?

Didn't children know more?

Did a child tell me only yesterday

we have to be good people

no matter what else happens?

How does he know this?

How will anyone carry on?

What might be gained?

Who needed power?

What was power?

The power to wash a dish?

To fold a cloth?

To place a book back on a shelf?

To have home still be there?

Where was the poet who wrote

Most of us would take our children over land?

Was it me? Who was I?

If someone killed someone else

could they ever again be alive?

Grief Tsunami

Thinking

how Palestinians

would have stopped everything

to feed you.

Please Look Closely

Where does terror come from?

        Possibly from people who are terrified.

        Or have been terrorized.

Why does it hurt more when the victims

        are boys on a beach?

They had the breath of the sea in their lungs.

        They were running, leaving footprints.

Does the word "innocent" have no bearing anymore?

        Depends on what you use it for.

Why can't the world see?

        The world can see.

            People with keys to bombers can't see.

"Investigation" is empty.

We will win. Be on top. No more shoddy little rockets from you

        second-rate folk.

Maybe they forget what it felt like

        to be collectively slaughtered.

We have the right. We right the wrong.

It's been going on so long they forget

what happened before.

Lonesome on the Earth

"I saw, as in a dream sublime,
the balance in the hand of Time."
—Henry Wadsworth Longfellow

And how far off was that hand?

Did it dwell inside every minute?

Over which continent

did it pass its steadying sweep,

was it a breeze after long days?

Why did we feel so lonesome

on the earth, in our own lives?

Longing for earlier selves,

or selves that never were?

Longing for our loved ones?

Something clearer in the eyes of babies had gone

missing in us now, some radiant gaze.

Before words, when shapes,

sounds, and reaching, defined.

For once an answer, not the endless asking.

Current Affairs

I don't want to be

one of those modern people

who reads about Gazans

being crushed wholesale

entire blocks

extended families

invisible kitchens

then continues scrolling.

We will not delete you.

We would give you

anything we have.

Your pain is not money.

Feel us from a far place.

Howling in darkness.

What are you supposed to?

No one should have to bear.

I love you so much I can smell

the garlic in your shirt,

the dirt on your shoes,

the smoke in your air.

In a Village in the West Bank

One little boy writing a book,
"making pictures for it too," he said over Zoom,
proud face bright as an apple in my screen.
"It's about a problem," he smiled shyly
in that occupied land where soldiers
sneak around at night
breaking into houses, chopping olive trees,
smashing lamps.
"A problem between spiders and ants." This sounded
refreshing, a problem not made by humans. He said
spiders and ants each want to dominate their corners,
not letting other species have space.
I didn't quite understand, since spiders
spin high-up webs and ants tunnel in the ground,
but he insisted on friction, something about vicinity.
They want the *whole* space.
I could see stone walls behind him.
Hear his parents speaking Arabic in the background,

spoon clinking a bowl. I felt homesick for my whole life.
Now he was whispering, other kids listening in,
scattered in villages around the West Bank
where my grandma once lived.
I knew exactly what their world looked and
smelled like, and wished to be with them
on that ground, stirring smoky coals in a *taboon.*
"But there's something the ants can do,"
he went on softly.
"So they don't all get killed. The spiders are stronger
than the ants, you know. So the ants *pretend*
to be spiders!"
What? How does an ant pretend to be a spider?
He showed reluctance to tell, being still immersed
in the making of his story, but gave a clue.
"It's an expression on the face. An ant makes his face
look like a spider's face. For safety.
Then they won't attack.
It's not that hard."

To the Americans Voting Against Ceasefire in Gaza

Baby Jesus prince of peace

is not happy with you people.

I know I promised never to speak

for Jesus again, but it's urgent.

Americans stringing up

Christmas lights,

bang the pans!

Who are you trying

to please, and why?

You can't say you want peace,

then look away.

If this were your girl, your boy,

sobbing with kitten, tattered blanket,

what would you do next?

Can you think that far?

If you can't, don't

celebrate my birthday.

I don't want you

at my party.

Beautiful Gaza

The people who live there made it feel
like home. They planted strawberries,
weeded fields,
carried little backpacks
to school.

You like to go places?
So did they.
But they couldn't
go far. They could travel to the next town
or camp if they were lucky. Sometimes
they blew up balloons
or cooked outside on open fires,
like a party.

There are many kinds of lucky.

I saw a video *Beautiful Gaza, My Home,*
narrated by a young girl.
TV stations might play that video

every day now. They owe this to

so many people.

Once, in days that felt more free,

we traveled from Egypt

up through Gaza on a public bus.

We had passports. We could go places.

The bus rattled mightily.

You lay in the back seat with malaria,

sweat pooling on your forehead,

bandanna tied around nose and mouth.

This was before everyone had masks.

Women and men who didn't even know you

stooped to offer water, wipe your brow.

This is what I remember of Gaza.

Beautiful fields.

The people wiped your brow.

Aziz

1.

You exist, you do not exist.

What a ridiculous state of affairs.

His best friend was killed sitting

on a bench beside him. He carried that bench

his entire life. A gentle-looking woman

blew a kiss to him from a bridge. He worried about

her future. *You were always here, but*

you are not here. Hard to explain the predicament of the

Palestinian, but he tried so hard to do so.

He connected his story. Native Americans, they knew.

He told the tale anywhere it was invited.

Respecting all people felt obvious. His friends

extended to the horizon.

He had friends he didn't know he had.

Never have I been glad he is no longer here

till now, when the poor thin millions of Gaza,

whom he loved so much, stagger through dust with

battered cook pots desperate for gruel.

What would this have done to him?

How would he have retained his smile?

2.

I heard a bird tweet the way my father used to chirp

stepping into a room with hope for the day.

He did a little dance with one hand and both feet

before sitting at the table. He waited for his tea to steep

and he waited to feel better and he waited for the world to

grow sane. He is gone now but omnipresent. Thank you

for knowing his song. This is spring's secret message

lasting longer than spring.

This is the mountain laurel.

The purple staggering scent at dawn.

No thirteen ways

to look at a genocide, they are all bad. If a boy's skin
crinkles with fire, bad. If a pregnant mother is crushed,
twice bad. If a little girl staggers two miles carrying
her bleeding sister, unspeakable. No words
from men in suits at safe microphones
will make it good. Crushed library,
words merging in ash. Crushed kitchen,
straw serving trays weep in secret. They had so much
left to do. No slogan about defense or intention feels true
to any of them. Stop now. Stop yesterday.
Fables of moral superiority long dissolved.
This child's cry is what you will be hearing when
somewhere, down the road in a lonely clean
room, you die.

Defense

Around our memories

we dig a moat of quietude.

What strawberries hear

when they are growing

under leaves.

You can't cross it.

You can't even

see it.

You can't burn it

with your firebombs.

When you strip the little children

of their skins,

a deeper child

in the mind of every

innocent

person

dives into the moat

weeping, privately,

for the lives

lost

and the people

abandoning their souls.

Vengeance

My mother told of a woman who ate so much her stomach
exploded. She told me this when I was three or four.

I think she read it in the newspaper. It was a very bad story to tell
a child. Whenever my tummy felt full, I worried,

placing both my hands on rounded abdomen to keep it calm.
Since we lived in days when children

were expected to clean their plates, this was also confusing. Now
I'm not even sure her story was true.

If so, why have we never heard of this happening again? My
mother was a fascinating complicated woman

filled with random facts on any topic you could imagine. I wish I
had asked her more about the stomach

before she died. Now I lie awake and miss her. Also I think about
vengeance, how long it takes for someone

to be satisfied they have hurt you more than you hurt them, they
have won.

On the other side of the earth, Israelis are starving Palestinians.
Beautiful, brown, brave, bony Palestinians.

They are shooting them as they stand in desperate lines for food.
My father used to say we are all cousins,

my Palestinian friend says it is more like brothers and sisters. I
realize many people do not get along with their

brothers or sisters. Nevertheless it will be hard to talk about only
one holocaust in the future. Currently it is

hard to sleep without imagining their cries. Hard to enjoy a large restaurant meal or a big bowl of noodles at

home. Once again, it is hard to feel full.

Thick Air

To recount details immediately after death,
(she looked peaceful, held his hand firmly),
repeat what someone said,
how the light changed, a necessary testament,
          This happened.
To absorb that *she left.*
Standing in the hall, her grandson felt a breeze.

Ritual we've all gone through—
weeks later you won't recall
exactly the grip, three white petals
that fell onto the table right after.
But now you must tell this
to every person who enters,
her eyelids flickered one last time
when we pledged our love.

It must be different in Gaza,
so many leaving at once,
under rubble, wreckage,

no soft beds, farewell glances,

only trauma and ruin for months.

People so hungry for a regular day.

Life already like death, everything gone

before you are.

Boys waving soup pots, crazed looks in their eyes.

Pink swaddled babies, supple faces

who never did anything bad.

Gone the fields, cars, kitchens. *Every one of them loved.*

This was a world, the only place

they were allowed to know.

They chopped carrots, grew mint.

Treasured books standing neatly on shelves.

Cats ate from this bowl. They liked plastic shoes.

So wrap the ravaged bodies, roll them in long lines.

Seventeen or forty from a family.

What scrap of final information might anyone report

to show their care? Such a shattering aberration.

Not enough time to say any prayer.

Throw Away

This person did not kill that person.

This person is a baby.

She had a notebook and a doll.

This person was in second grade.

She was doing well.

For a few months she

whimpered every morning,

but now she'd grown brave.

This boy hoarded seashells

in a cardboard box that once held

French fries. This girl had a map.

Her grandpa kept books

from 1947 by his bed.

He couldn't remember

not having them.

Please

Sometimes I say No to no one,
says the blonde girl clutching
her brother's stroller
on a Princeton street.
Sweet morning plush with green.
Was she addressing me?
I lined up for coffee and oats,
spoke too brightly to strangers
who didn't reply. So it's nice to hear
such a clear bell of a voice
lighting the air beside
the sleeping bookshop
and the fancy faucets store.
More time with that girl
would suit me right now.
I say Yes to everyone.
How can it be? A corner kiosk
for magazines greets us all
so tenderly.

For Gaza

"When does the grief lessen?
When will people stop treating other people as disposable!?
What do we do till then?"

—Danusha Laméris

The children are still singing.

They need & want to sing.

Carrying cats to safe places.

Holding what they can hold.

Red hair brown hair yellow.

They will wear the sweater

someone else once wore.

They will hope for something tasty.

You won't be able to own them.

Their spirits fly to safer worlds.

They planted seashells in the sand.

They never committed a crime.

A president pardons turkeys.

He pardons his own son.

He doesn't pardon children.

The children are still singing.

Tunnel

Why should I have
this big wooden table
laden with roses and books
while children stagger through
ruin and dirt? Crushed,
the daily word
undeserved.

Lost in mystery's tunnel,
some wander beauty,
others navigate disaster.

What Does It Mean
To Be a Palestinian Now?
article in the mail.
It means what it always meant,
we're proud, invisible,
trying really hard—
and sad.

Email Gift from Naomi, Israeli Poet

People in Israel gather in a square
to read the names of dead children, babies.
Pronouncing them slowly, each syllable
a tuft of hair, ages in holy succession.
Eight months, seven years. Hebrew speakers
shaping Arabic rolled from the throat,
rich with respect. Why can't this be
our only way? *Two years, eleven months.*
  Hendia Janan Bilal.
    Rafik Mahmoud Darwish Abdullah.
Blanket wrapped bodies,
perfect ear ripped
from the perfect head.
What did the mothers do next?

Catholic ex-president on Delaware beach
staring east. May he imagine them every day.
May they be the wind ruffling him.
Don't stop. He didn't stop.

His own lost daughter had my same name,

same as the Israeli poet who sent this video.

His granddaughter, recently a mother, too.

Our name is HUMAN

(Holy Mary Mother of God).

The video lasts eleven hours plus.

Voice Message from Gaza

She sings, whispers, prays.

She can see the moon, not yet set,

the morning breeze feels almost normal.

In the background, fighter jets,

she doesn't mention them.

One palm tree persists.

When she cries, she apologizes.

Her favorite student was incinerated

one month ago.

On his way to have coffee with her...

he was just walking over.

He'd been down to the beach to take

deep breaths. So handsome

he could have been a film star.

He posted his mint and tomato plants

on Instagram. You can see them.

Recently he told her

he wanted to write stories

anyone could understand,

for people who'd never been to Gaza

or trapped. He knew

she would smile. This had been her job,

encouraging students.

He knew she'd be proud.

This was something he could really do.

Gheed's Voice

In your voice, no sharp edge,
or hint of bitterness, only
the soft hills and slopes of a field
billowing neat rows of grapes,
subtle patches of strawberry leaves,
the rumple of sand as a normal wave
comes and goes again. How blessed
any normal exchange. You say,
"messy, a little bit," to describe
conditions. Your voice a soothing
breeze, a prompt toward consolation,
the gentle voice nurses use after surgeries
to bring a patient back to consciousness,
a voice encouraging scared students,
comforting mothers, softening bad news.
You were raised to encourage, transforming
one word to another as power,
stretching boundaries for others, there was
no chapter on annihilation in your plan.

Voice Message from Gaza

You are so nice to think of me.

Thank you for worrying about us.

We send you care. We are still here.

Mish-mish is scared of loud sounds.

She hides under a pillow.

You would not want to see this.

Every place crushed—

everything we needed for our lives.

Last night some people

walked as families

to the one still-standing café

rumored to have spinach pies,

and were crushed. Forty of them.

Unfortunately.

People eating pies.

Each day I make care packages of

hygiene products, socks.

It's incredible

to be treated worse than animals,

small sacks of bread pitched

to a large crowd, everyone starving,

scrambling to catch some.

The soldiers laugh

as they throw it.

We love our animals.

That is a difference.

And in the United States

The Jewish and Arab students
Californians, New Yorkers
Texans, New Mexicans
gathered together in small tents
on the lawns of their schools
to sing *Life! Life! Stop killing*
one another! Stop sending bombs
to slaughter innocent people!
Stand up for one another!
And for this
they got in trouble.

❧

I walked the University of Texas campus
one day after National Guardsmen on horseback
arrested dozens of students for peaceful protest.
Yellow police blockades felt like
giant X's on a test. WRONG!
The line at the falafel truck stretched
two blocks long.

In Ohio, a second-grader handed me a "cultural passport" and said, "We are doubling down on diversity here!"

One Day in August

A Democratic senator

who used to seem smart

but has stood lockjaw with Israel's

slaughter and starvation

turns her head the tiniest bit

to say

Palestinians

may be human beings after all

deserving of a few rights

definitely a breakfast

now and then.

For this

people celebrate.

Dear Gheed

WhatsApp delivers to me the frothy heart
in your coffee all the way across the sea.
You say it gives you hope. It makes me cry.
You're grateful for a new blue hoodie
found in its wrapper under a rock,
but worry who never got to wear it.
What happened to the flowered blouses
folded neatly in your cupboard?
You dream of stacking rolled scarves.
You liked giving things away.
Remember when the angry mother
entered your classroom
mad at her son for not doing dishes
before he came?
She pointed him out at the table.
He squirmed. She said in Arabic,
Stories! Stories! All he talks
about is stories!

You said, *Sit down dear.*

Write us a story about dishes.

Maybe dishes like to take a rest too.

I loved how the students loved you.

2

"We need our petit absorptions like campstools in the wilderness"

—Jack Kerouac

Legacy

My dad did not buy hummus in a tub.

He stirred and stirred

the floating chick peas in a simmering pot,

dropping moons of garlic into the pool,

he hovered in the kitchen singing

in Arabic, humming a lemony homesick song,

he mashed and mashed

then mixed his dollop of tahini,

spoons of olive oil, into the creamy

blend, his happiness had no beginning or end.

And I was his daughter.

Ritual

Mikey and Miriam

Up and down the house

on her walker

after Antiques Road Show

Oh no

she'd say

I can't do it

My poor stiff legs

Not tonight

I promise tomorrow night

Please not tonight

You said

Yes yes yes

It's good for you

caring coach

steady hand

center of her back

Come on

Few more steps

I'm with you

You can do it

Your legs are happier

Feel that?

You'll get stronger

this way

Look at you go!

Attentive

When our parents were still on earth, daily we asked—
are they okay? How might we help? No one
on earth feels that way about us. A cat
watches our moves so closely, hypnosis may be
involved, but our joy does not seem
his concern. He wants to race outside, smell a raccoon,
shoot back in. I don't recognize my country.
Is it helping us?
Once I took my mother to a doctor
who compared her knees to car tires
and said they were too old to be fixed.
Insulted, she did not want another minute
with this boor. To change the mood, she said,
What's something we like to eat
that we rarely make?
Popovers, I said. You made them once,
then never again.
The way they puff into pillows,

disregarding common ingredients,

so everyone says, Wow!

Let's have a little bit of that right now.

Tomorrow the Purple Building Goes Down

It's been empty such a long time.

We'd never before seen the ancient white stones

hiding under the stucco facing.

But that color helped us live our lives.

Ozark Birdsong

in memory, Paulette Jiles

Everything humans have done—

and still,

they're singing.

Homesick for the Word Humanity

1

Wasn't it a cotton shirt you wore every day,
tattered relic,
soft veteran of yard labor?
You could nap in it and feel comfortable.
Didn't we need shirts like that
more than nicer shirts?
Brown T with frayed collar,
gray tank with mended patch.

2

It's undersung, the far side
of being young. Also, sadness.
Sometimes it gives you space.
But the word *cruelty*, so palpable now,
popular with a shockingly large crowd,
feels lost when the sun goes down.
This word can never own anything
though it pretends.

It has never felt the preciousness of twilight,

or leaves crackling underfoot, in the dark.

Desk

1

I hover at the edges of your lonely desk.
Strange trinkets in drawers, broken prayer-beads,
seashell with a face painted on its back,
Palestinian keychain. When people say to me,
"There are no Palestinians," I say,
"Wish you could have known my dad."
Wish his deep eyes could have stared into yours.
Wish you could sit here at this sacred
abandoned spot and feel the longing
in these wooden legs.

2

Thank you for a path, at least.
A path paved with words
through forests of incomprehension.
You knew it was fine to look back,
to carry what remained unresolved.
There was no rush. And here we are,

floating in your old rooms,

with a small turquoise Egyptian head

hawked at the pyramids for two piastres.

Suspended with the sounds of passing cars,

which you disliked. I speak to your tree's

roots poking out of parched soil

beyond your window, and the ways

we all failed, and you kept trying.

Too Muchness

No one mentions overpopulation now.

It's been replaced by walls, and war.

Malvina Reynolds sang "little boxes on a hillside,"

but people kept building them. Stripping the land.

Seemed impressive Malvina started singing in her sixties

and caught on. Never too late.

Some days now

it feels too late.

A boy wrote "Everything was old

before I was born."

A room holding little, but carefully placed.

Ten minutes of luminosity, wider than a day.

It does not have to be

more, and more, and more.

Flags

Why are all the flags at half-mast?

I ask the boys in the back seat.

One says, War?

Trump?

I love them so much.

I say, Probably because

of the Texas floods and all the people

who washed away.

Silence, silence, silence.

Think of Me

He said, I'll be calm, careful and cool
as the other side of a pillow. I'll lay low
and try not to bother you. I'll hide my woes
in a sock, then tie the top like a pirate. I'll go into
the jungle. I'll be far away as a human can be.

When you think of me, think of someone
who had plans, who was shaken up,
whose house cracked, whose shelves fell over.
Think of the lover with no one in his grasp.
Think of the blue air letter sheets we used to
fold and seal, to send to one another in
different countries, when news still had a
hopeful flare around it, and words were lit
with sunbeams a child would draw,
in a painting for school.

Voice of America

The Voice of America transported us to Karachi, Damascus, Islamabad, Abu Dhabi, Dhaka. We sat in circles on wooden floors, wore white flower garlands on beaches. Were welcomed. Spent birthdays beneath mosquito nets. Rode in rickshaws. Stirred curries. A monkey climbed through a window in south India to lift the lid of a pot. We met photographers, artists, poets, children with blossoms tucked behind their ears, a journalist with a vendetta against the United States till he heard my name and it was the same name as his and we became friends for years. He wrote different stories. He changed his tune. We made so many friends, all our tunes changed. They became bigger tunes, tie-dyed scarves wrapped as turbans, vines climbing a wall in Lahore, a new friend saying, Americans don't have to write about hard things, your lives are easier, but we have to write about hard things, because it is all we have. Hey there, I am reaching out to you. We have hard things too. We met a man in a wheelchair who flew so majestically in his lines the whole room cried. I kissed a distinguished elder on his cheek in a country where you don't do that and the world did not end. And right now I would kiss every one we ever met and dined with and listened to because the Voice of America will no longer connect us, but there are some things you don't forget.

Dear Children

We do not wake up hating.

We do not wake up better than anyone else.

If someone says something ugly,

we don't say it too. Stand back.

Remember a cat curled on your feet.

We brush our hair with hope.

Yesterday we learned three things:

Neptune is the coldest planet.

They used to say Pluto, but Pluto got reclassified.

Two times nine equals eighteen and somehow

that is easier than two times eight. Some numbers

feel like friends. Would you rather be even or odd?

We do not want more than our neighbors have,

because how could we enjoy it? If you have a scooter,

I will take a scooter. I do not need a rocket launcher.

If you eat peaches, I will have peaches. Did you see

the sad man at the corner holding a sign?

His sign is different, did you notice? Bring him a

hot biscuit, an apple. We need

to visit the Botanical Garden to see

what really changed.

Living With It

When the boy says,

I'm thinking about the past

and you ask, what past,

you know he will say "dad"

and the day shift into

a lower key, even if wind

is brisk, with

feathered clouds.

No way around this. He's gone

for all of you. Weather changes

no matter what

anyone does.

When the boy says, disbelieving,

How could anyone be elected president again

after so many various venomous crimes?

you think, there's the headline.

Venomous? What a perfect word!

Where did you get it? He shrugs.

How long again will he be there? Covering his face
to hear, *Till you're twelve.* Twelve feels
far away when you're eight.

So, we're lucky to have houses, right?
Lucky to have food and feet,
schools and beds.
To stir biscuits in a big white bowl,
then knead them with our hands
and wait for them to rise,
even when we can't.

Tears, Appropriate

Am I bigger than gravity? he asked so long ago,
dragging up the steep slope
to our temporary Hawaiian home

past wrapped parcels of rubbish and
ruffled tangerine trees and
everything else that did not see us.

Yes, I said, tugging him.
I mean,
No.

I wanted to be bigger than temporary.
Circulating seasons of wind
and rain, to hold vowels

close under a tongue till they dissolved.
Melodious names of streets become second nature,
maybe the daily song he sang about earth and sky

in beautiful Hawaiian language was also mine.

Is it bigger than the moon? It's huge. *Can you put it*

in a pocket? Tell me!

From a high rim over the city

lights/glass/traffic/construction cranes/

questionable glitter. Beyond that—

the blue that solved it all. Space

and waves making everything

temporary, but true.

Always I ached for earlier times,

Robert Louis Stevenson writing

under a banyan tree. Quietude of small pools,

two giant turtles sunning on a beach

without turning their heads.

In those days

before all the harder days to come,

his hair was long, he said, *Let's speak*

only Hawaiian for the whole evening, okay?

But he would have been
talking to
himself.

In those days he would still hold my hand
and thirty years later
when my mother was dying

we held hands again at her bedside as
gravity pinned us and breath slowed
to a halting wisp, then fell. Sounding like a shelf

of memories dropping forever
to the bottom of the sea.
O please! An island far from the fact of it.

The nurse acknowledged our behaviors
on a form, wrapped a white towel
beneath my mother's chin, and just like that,

gravity shifted—the one person you always
tried to please, now gone. I wished you could
remember that song.

Driver

Your postage sized face in the red bus
lumbering around our Sheridan corner
comforts a slow-moving pedestrian,
or quiet homebody clipping vines.
You are steady at the wheel,
staring straight ahead, we could climb on
if we wanted to, be carried safely
to another part of town, another life.
Only rarely you raise your hand to say Hi.
Maybe it's against the rules. I always raise mine though,
as I still do to trains, like a child, and sometimes
you toot, and there's a moment of connection,
and I still smile. Where do you live,
are you sick of your route?
We were young and happier once,
we rode the bus all the time,
south on Blanco Road,
or all the way to Wisconsin,

awakening achy, staring out the windows at a
blurred field, while you, mysterious beautiful you,
remained miraculously alert,
sure of destinations, eyes pinned to pavement
and the coming day.

Dear Bobcats

We gather together now as true family
instead of regular family
because we are far flung brave creatures
and these are wild days.
I know people don't see us very often.
We will not curl on your feet to sleep, but
will accompany all your dreams.
Even if you see only one of us
in your whole lifetime.
Like the foxes, or single sleek coyote you witnessed
running up a major thoroughfare in your city,
then blink! Gone.
We, the armadillos and snakes,
in the Year of the Snake, will be recognized.
We root and rumble, curl in a hollow.
We find our quiet ways.
Our numbers shrink, but we don't do math.
We persist. You too must live like this.

Everyone Before Us

at Tassajara

I touch the chair
where my mother sat reading
stare at the bridge she crossed
the bench she favored
This sacred gravel
we walked on another year
stone seat by window
pool of light
Where is the man who tended
his wife so gently?
Young couple from Santa Cruz
grieving their child?
Friends crisscrossed
over steaming platters
Suzuki Roshi memorial
on high hillside
silences we once knew still with us

girder and glaze

Where is the

bullfrog

during the day?

Air Mind

I'm going to air out my brain the way
Germans advise leaving a rumpled bed
wide open an hour before making it.
Don't fret around politicians
to start our mornings. They'll go their own ways
whatever we think. What would it be like
to live four whole years without
thinking of them?
How much room?
So far my opinion meant nothing
to a single one, and what about yours?
Reams of futility,
Zendo of emptiness.
One loud mockingbird in the laurel,
soft light lifting,
poking into thought.

Green House

To be given space

awakened to space

wider ways of being

openings you hadn't realized

were missing

in mind or sight

a moment lifts

everything you gripped

relinquished

Some houses say

I am bigger than I look

invite a pause

from any angle

sheen of cabinet

surprising green wall

Some reckon with

your issues

In some, you forget

your issues

Some buildings

turn you inside out

Keep one room empty

for all we can't cure

Medicare Wellness Test

Can you tie your shoe, sing a lullaby,
draw the face of a clock?
How many times did you miss being younger this week?
How many young people listened when you spoke?
Is there anyone young who still loves you?
Do you have sad thoughts?
Do you need help making a meal?
Do you walk around your neighborhood
thinking of everyone that is gone?
Are you unconditionally opposed
to building a new stadium?
Do you miss the Institute of Texan Cultures
with a fervor that is almost strange?
Do you have trouble remembering
your name, your mother's name,
the name of your second grade teacher,
your shoe size? Do your neighbors
humor you? Have you always had
a fervent desire to leave things

on people's doorsteps? What is that connected to?

Do you need to be liked?

Do you miss parking meters?

What do you do in your spare time?

Is time your friend? Did you draw that clock yet?

Did you give it two hands?

Did you have a desire to make them look like your own?

At the Book Festival

No bombs were thrown for varying opinions, no grenades
cast onto words, we felt sane for a day, mingling,
as of old, with people we did or did not know, listening
in unison, greeting and hugging,
finding another room, tent,
Italian crème cake after lunch for energy,
buying a book for its title alone, not feeling stuck
or lost, on the brink of collapse,
or scared of anyone else, or worried, not a bit.
Sitting next to people we did not know,
everyone smiled. At the Book Festival we were
wildly wealthy, truly democratic.

Cathy

After thirty years,
my high school senior English teacher
returned some of my papers
in a large brown envelope.
Startling mail.
Nice comments though.
Her suggestions for improvement
now struck me
as profoundly generous.
Please meet me for lunch,
I wrote back.
At the seafood dive,
she said, *Call me Cathy.*
So strange—we had become
the same age.

I Miss Myself When I'm Not Here

Connor, Age 4

1

Once we rode elevators
without fear.
Never thought being next to people
in a small box
could be a luxury we'd miss.
The child asked others where
they were going—
That's really high!

Once our own father took us to the airport
to watch people arriving,
departing. Sometimes he said,
"Welcome!" to strangers.
It moved him.
He had tears in his eyes.
There was no security.
He was homesick for a homeland.

We are homesick for a homeland.

2

Even on Halloween night, traipsing

his neighborhood of goblins and ghouls,

Connor looked up, took a deep breath, and said,

"Oh Momo, look at the stars."

Quarantine

A neighbor said he moved to a bucket inside a cave.
I opened a box sealed for twenty years
to find letters written to a remote satellite person.
Who was this Marjorie sending missives from Alaska?
Now was the time to think more deeply:
children of Gaza, trapped in tiny rooms,
beautiful people camped, exhausted,
along the Rio Grande,
patting masa, stirring beans, on a fire made of sticks
inside a ring of stones, no idea what came next.
Could we ever know the hardest stories
when we had the same house keys
so many years?

We Could Not Know

No, we could not know.

Our tiny antennae reached out, trembling,

hoping for a message, clear advice on how to help.

We were stunned

by the smallness of our worlds.

Here is the edge of your street,

three scrappy leaves. From which tree did they fall?

Here, the wrapper from someone else's gum.

I could pick up trash without seeing anyone.

No one would breathe on us

in the iron chair back of the house,

beside the bamboo. Machines to connect us

to the outside world. And now we might eat applesauce

from cups, sort pantries for relics, feel the quiet

settling down. Consider it a preview

for the future

when no one will answer

the number we call.

The Road Between San Antonio and Comstock, Texas

I think of it as a bloodline, clean thread

stretching west, the mind emptying so gently

as it ranged farther from billboards,

chains, farther from access roads,

exits, deeper into sky,

that road is why I love this state,

despite politics, pronouncements,

the boy called Cody in Comstock who wrote me,

a year after I visited his class,

Basically poetry changed everything, it made me see

where I was, could you please come back

and stay forever? Finding his letter again

thirty years later, looking him up

to learn he died young,

cowboy hat over his downturned face,

I want to say,

Your roads are still stretching outwards,

the fields you walked through, we are here

soaking in the mystery of time, trapped in our little houses,

scared of a virus, feeling connected through spaces,

all these new ways, and I do remember you.

Michigan

Dark fields, quiet roads

between airport and anywhere—

thrumming of

wheels.

When it snows

in April,

we eat hot porridge,

hot fish at Catholic Fish Fry,

try to remember

what keeps us warm.

Tulips poking up

red heads.

Give up your guilt!

my friend said.

Some days, it's stitching me

together. Guilt, its miserable needle,

traces of rust

on the sad cloth.

Daily Dialogue with the Dalai Lama

You say, *the only way to stop terror is through altruism.*

Thank you, we're trying to be decent in small ways.

You say, *compassion is an aspiration.*

Leaders, listen up! Since when do

only Popes and Dalai Lamas aspire?

This appetite for domination, destruction

is not on our menu.

To develop patience, you need someone

who willfully hurts you.

Palestinians got that one down.

We grow in kindness when our kindness is tested.

Sometimes my daily Dalai calendar

speaks right to the moment.

Sometimes it's high school.

I'm never lonely. We're all humans.

Old friends pass away, new friends appear.

Yes, we have been tackling problems

nonviolently for quite a while.

The world's acute suffering

accumulating

like a craze, a terrible trend.

Stress is simply the brain's way

of signaling something is important.

We are living landmark days.

World Ocean Day

Waves keep circulating

new hopes

You're not here to feel them

Three African drummers lugging

large hand drums show up

at the poetry tent

Take it away friends

My words got lost

in the wind

Gulls think we're dull

Time loosening its grip

going where

it already is

Maybe a choice

to be empty?

to be vast?

History

"I haven't seen him in years. No, we're not in touch."

What made us so angry, way back when?

What caused you to slam a door,

kick a hole through it, drive away fast

shouting insults?

We were people awakening.

We were young, lean,

still had dark hair.

Now would someone just post it or shoot?

Do you ever feel we fell off the map?

Maybe the road was always ending

and no one would tell us. We just had to

disappear.

I'm sorry.

No, I'm not.

Red Legs

for the Chukar partridge

We saw you in India, dipping down to the tank,
as everyone called it,
right before the sun slipped away.
You walked cheerfully toward water,
oblivious to bigger birds, red legs confident
on sand.
Chukar, how have you come so far?
Oman to Palestine, Dead Sea,
even Hawai'i, your tail has only 14 feathers.
What could you teach the crazy humans
about co-existence,
chuck chuck chukar chukar,
your chant of peace,
maybe your heart has 144 hopes.
We need your wisdom drenching us in our desert.
I'm lonely for everything I believed as a child.
We can be friends with anyone. Wars are dumb.

Even though you are hunted in Washington and Oregon,
our own supposedly civilized gun-loving land,
you still make a stand there.
You are "relatively unaffected by loss of habitat."
Good thing.
Bless the Gazans please,
expected to conduct their days in a heap of rubble.
"When disturbed, you prefer to run rather than fly."
Bless their own thin legs.
Make the ground their sky.

Vigilance

For years, my friend cared for her father.
Delivered snug, knee-high socks,
tugged rug to artful angle on his floor.
She arranged paintings,
refreshed the fruit
in his bowl.
They attended every
traveling musical
at the Majestic
because her father
loved show tunes so much.
She called him
more than once a day.
And now they are both dead.
Even her husband
who was sick the whole time
yet assisted everybody,
is dead.

All these people
who traded so much care
are dead. Their dog
outlived them though,
sniffing old friends curiously
as if we each became
an unspoken language,
vaguely familiar, but who?
The dog nearly knows.
But with none of them
here anymore, who are we?
Could this be the hum we feel
walking outside
right before dawn,
softening sky,
secret breath
rising from ancient cypress,
white crane called into air?

For Our Neighbors

Stolen Buddha Head, we meditate on your grace,
consider how you must be gazing
at a Flea Market stall now,
or the walls of a truck, wondering how you got there,
as we wonder every day about our world, what happened
to that calm place we dreamed, where did this jostling
and cruelty come from? Buddha, I admit
I worried about you
before you were stolen. Because you sat
in the front yard visible to all.
If this precipitated your departure,
as someone once suggested
(worry a bad thing might happen, it more likely might),
then I too am at fault. You helped me. You held a note.
Jane planted red flowers in front of you. We watered them.
Please guard our disappeared best dreams.

Glories

1

Hard to see, being in the center of the frame,

pressured mornings, game dates, birthday bash,

dental appointment, project pending,

poster board, lost scissors, stuck bottle of glue.

Have a good day darling, give me a hug, don't forget

your lunch money there on the seat, be careful,

call if you feel sick again, check the lost & found for your

jacket, your notebook, your hat, your shoe.

Hard to see this is the sweet spot, juicy flesh of the peach.

Later in day, driving back to school again

through afternoon's steamy press, waiting for just one

person to emerge from crowd,

slide hand into yours,

this is the hinge, the text, and everything else

the margin. And it is a big margin.

Such a long silence coming.

Elementary schools at dawn,

crossing guards in yellow belts

shouting proudly,

Signs down!

as if they have great power,

cars will stop,

everything will stop,

they are telling the truth.

2

Never underestimate the glory

of visiting your parents

even when they're fighting.

Even when they treat you as

a referee, a moderator

for their lifelong debate,

even when you have to step outside

to get some air, and they're still arguing

when you come back in.

Unhappy you missed

a few crucial points,
they're ready to catch you up,
hoping to get you on their sides,
both sides, DNA swirling.

As a kid you'd go outside
and hike in a drainage ditch
just to get some peace.
Even when you say,
I'm not coming back here
till you get some counseling,
you know that will never happen,
you'll be back in two weeks,
they need you, they always needed
an audience, they were both stars,
you were the front row
and someday you will miss them forever.

Lonesome

"...the passing away of companions which constitutes the true tragedy of old age."

—Buddha, Karen Armstrong

When neatnik poet jazzman Roberto left,
you made empty spaces in his memory.

When Rose slipped away, who on earth
could you tell that crazy story to now?

When Kathleen took off in secret,
pretending she wasn't leaving,
what could you ever believe?
Now who would say, you look bad in that,
take it off?

When Sharon, when Wendy...
each friendship its own country
of fun, hope, disarray.

And the question that trails us,
what did we ever give them
for everything they gave?

Calling Back

for W.S. Merwin

The last time we ever
spoke by phone
things blurring by then
words farther apart
drifting syllable threads
What's that? you'd say
asking me to repeat
But how are you really?
knowing you missed Paula too much
to mention it
We traded words tenderly
your trees
our palm tree in Texas you had planted
so many years ago
when we all had easier times
walking hidden roads
You carried it in your pocket
Baby palm from Gonzales

saying it would grow waist-high

William, it is twenty feet tall!

Silences felt lit

soft evening light on my end

afternoon birds on yours

In the gaps

your breathing calm as ever

You said *Ah well* the way

you always did

You held a note

still William

in every way

I thanked you for

encouraging me

always to speak to the dead

out loud

You said they might even

answer sometimes

in ways that might be

important

surely this had been true

already

and would be even more true

later

When we hung up

so reluctantly on my side

I sat at the wooden table

trying to rise

thinking that might be

the last time I ever heard

your gentle voice

in my ear

Maybe our giant palm

was bowing down right then

When the phone dinged

your number again

it seemed a mistake

for sure

You'd always said

you hated telephones

But your elegant voice
that had traveled so many miles
said so many poems
helped so many people
feel more at home in words
than on earth
was right there
firmly asking
Could we talk some more?

3

"The Mystery never leaves you"
—John O'Donohue

Airport Announcement, San Antonio

Would the passenger

who left

a bucket of stones

with a candle

stuck in them

PLEASE return

to the security checkpoint?

Maine

Three sentences

in the sky

flush left

diminishing lengths.

Last time I was here

you were alive

❧

The world did not do

what we wanted it to do.

We kept looking at plants

and trees for guidance.

Comfort zones continuously challenged.

We kept making metaphors involving

sky, horizon, waves.

Another Boy Told Me

McNay Museum, San Antonio, Connor James, Age 5

1

If lightning strikes this deer sculpture,
will it fall over?
Why do artists paint naked bodies so much?
And the sculptures too.
They're all nude, ha ha.
That whole wall is nude!
I thought that statue was moving!
This is made out of string!
In the video where the ice melts in the glass
and the pear gets mold on it,
the apricots don't get mold.
Because they aren't cut, you know.
You thought it was a painting!
How could you?
Didn't you see the bubbles were moving
from the melting ice?

How long did the artist wait for the mold?
This could happen
on your table at home
right now.
Can you believe an artist
made a whole bunch of people
from Cheez Doodles? People standing
and sitting around like at a party.
When some of them started moving,
I almost fainted.
We need to stay here a while.
They might do something else.
What if the glasses float off the table?
Is there a motion detector?
When John Baldessari crosses his arms
and says, "I am Making Art,"
does he mean all the time or just in that video?
Look how he lifts one hand, then the other hand.
Then he raises his arms.
I am raising my arms too.

Can I paint when I get home?

I feel like I need to paint.

2

If you could have one thing in this museum

what would it be?

I take that—

No, I take that!

It's hard to decide!

Jesus looks like he's crying.

His eyes are wet.

How could this painting be 500 years old?

That means Jesus has been crying

for 500 years?

I like Georgia O'Keefe,

I really like her orange sky.

But her other painting

is more great.

I'm having better thoughts now.

I'm looking out the window.

It looks like a painting out there.

Can we go back to the Infinity Room

one more time?

"Falling Man" by Max Beckmann

1

What made a man topple in one
of Max Beckmann's last paintings
cannot now be remembered or described.
We could speculate
he slipped. Something pushed him.
He was on the edge for years.
He was all of us, don't even try.
If we had asked what was going on in days before,
he might have replied, Nothing, as children say
mournfully, once they've started school.
Or perhaps, I tried to leap beyond the fires
to save myself. Soaring into infinity,
some think, or a foretaste of the future,
but we see a man deep dive to his demise.
Buildings on both sides roar
from within, curtains, plants,
shivering flames, gulping
every inch of what was a room.

Smoke roils thickly around his plunging feet.
Beckmann could make smoke be clouds,
be thoughts, the weight of tangled dream.
These large sturdy feet might almost be
striking a dance pose. But they are upside down.
Consider everywhere they walked, and the man's
large capable hands, but what use?
A black wheel hovers to the left, he doesn't grab it,
Beckmann's wife called it a balcony
from a strange angle,
but our man is past steering or pausing.
Airplanes, boats,
hopeful means of travel,
float in the background, sky
merging with sea.
Once our man went places and returned.
He walked as a human—
no need for speed.
One plunge and all that's left are
flashing streams of thought—

in a moment to be gone.

But are they gone?

2

"Stop," she said. My mother would not
let me read aloud the final chapter of her
Beckmann biography because she knew
what happened in it. After all he had witnessed,
suffered, to move to St. Louis,
two happy years in a calm studio, an art school,
inspiring lives... her paintings look
like his. He called her his most "simpatico" student.
She didn't know the word. To me this seems
the greatest gift one might ever receive.
But she tells me only when she is dying.

People fell in German, Spanish, Arabic,
all over the world people fell, in the wars,
in the dark alley she'd grown up in, before art
encircled and held her so she didn't hit the ground.
Soaking in *something not yourself* was the way free,

expanding the mind, letting art be your compass,
your glide.

My mother could not bear to feel her
dearest teacher step out for a morning walk
across Central Park and fall.
His wife Quappi wrote
he was "freed of the horrors
and beauties of life on earth."
Swoops of oil remain.
Complete as anthems. Mysterious as days.

3

Your child dies and
you plummet off the roof too.
You will keep falling through
hours, months, anniversaries,
the unexpected thunder tilt of any moment
where he's suddenly
standing in the door.

How precious, the door.

Or—his voice plunges
into your ongoing sorrow—
what he would have said.
These little plaid pants. They traveled far
and weren't new when he got them.
Where do they go?

What was going on inside
you couldn't know.
Who was steering the wheel.
As a child, his future
loomed, gleaming, gracious,
long and bright as the sky behind
everyone upright, bigger than you were.
He would outlive all you shared.

But this will not be.
Find comfort in the Falling Man
whose face we can't see,
the mystery we're stuck with,
the thick arms so much

like his own. We want to stand

beneath the Falling Man

and catch him. Out walking,

we feel boys walking alongside us,

girls too, and ancestors, and the man with the brush,

Max.

Speak to the flaming silence,

the endless regret, but remember things

which do not plummet—

memory, color, love.

I should remember more than I do.

I might have noticed more than I did.

Beckmann's turquoise slash of fabric,

Beckmann's blue.

Smaller than a Mouse

We demonstrated on a steaming day,

carrying signs,

five hundred thousand people

in the streets of New York

saying no to war,

gathering crowds for blocks and miles,

crush and press of world's religions

and secular codes, multi-flavored

WE SHALL NOT KILL

and the next day our story,

the story of saying no to war,

was written up in a three-sentence news item

on the back of the front section of the *New York Times*

smaller than the story of a mouse found

in a chain restaurant soup.

This is the truth.

Hiss

Good thing you said
the iron's soft breath
was your favorite sound
of childhood.

You'd lie on the rug
next to me
reading out loud
as I flattened the tablecloths,
your daddy's shirtsleeves,
pant legs,
afternoon light steaming us
on. It felt cozy, you said,
like a song you feel better
just hearing.

Good thing you told me
because now that you're gone,
what other reason would I have
to make anything smooth?

Old Friend

"I am sure sorrow will
follow you until death."

Late at night, her text pings through.
It's true, but?

We stood up together
on the brink of our lives.

I was in the hospital
when her first baby was born.

Now, spring billowing,
I navigate my daily pool of gloom.

Arrange your five deflating basketballs
under the lonely net.

I always loved the honesty
of old friends.

And the Elk Went Running Past at Sundown

"The ground beneath your feet is not stable,"

said a Grand Tetons National Park sign

and you thought, for once someone tells the truth.

Shine

What image shall I carry?
Your finest face
rests in a cradle of leaves.
You're funny, Mom—
your biggest compliment.

Mostly I wanted you safe,
happy, as in the Buddhist chant,
the mother protecting
her only child.

This wild vacancy…
I batter against
the sides of any space now
since you're all space.

Care takes other shapes.
    What to plant?
    Who to tend?
Why does

the quiet old janitor of
Central School in Ferguson
keep coming to mind?
He haunted me.
He never spoke.
For years he carried a sponge
on a long stick, dipping it
a hundred times
into a bucket, day after day,
after everyone left,
erasing blackboards
to an empty shine.

Marfa

A departed boy now owns all his ages at once.
He is 15, 10, 5, joyous,
sketching graphs at poetry readings,
small arrows pointing to
"really boring" or "slightly better"
selections. "Seems like it's almost over"
brought 4 stars.

I jolt awake at 3 every night
for the "really worst" thoughts.

We can't believe he'll never be
hopping into the car again,
dragging golf clubs to Fort Worth,
shooting his famous three pointer
toward the net from the corner
of the yard.

When morning comes,
who wants to rise?

Rise—why?

A brain whirls, spins in its socket.
Not ready for coffee, unable to comfort itself.
I feel my father wailing for the children of Gaza
who never hurt anyone in their lives. Wailing for
his grandson, who hugged a chicken and
made him laugh. In the stars,
the dark, a gentle man sobs for the universe.
Maybe they're all together now—I wish.

Why, if we were so happy in Marfa,
have we never gone back in 20 years?

Days of Cheer

Sometimes they passed so quietly we missed them.
No one was killing anyone anywhere in the world,
was there ever that day?
Children enjoyed their lessons,
ran wide circles on the playground,
sang in Hawaiian a lilting phrase
about blue waves kissing sky.
Why didn't we stop everything
and stay there? Parents
as blessed sidekicks
to the child.
Why didn't we tell one another,
this will be the only place
we ever want to go?

Dearest Son

At least when I die I won't have to be sad
about missing you. We're already in practice.
And at least this isn't the first year you are gone,
that year was more shocking. What did we even do.
We may have collapsed in the silverware drawer
for entire days or lived as puffs of vapor.
But now you're not first in the exit line.
I guess that softens the blow though considering
so many other grieving fathers and mothers
does not. Please be nice to all the boys
from Gaza who look like you.
We can never claim to understand anything
ever again. Now we could have rain, a fat rose,
a bowl of soup, an apple tart, jazz in the background,
and still feel entirely lost. It's not like you left
and the world continued. It's like you left
and you were the world.

“Those Who Knew Me Knew Me Well”

Then the words “Beloved Friend” on a tombstone
without dates.
There’s a haunting in this. Because we don’t get to know
the person’s name, how long they lived, or in which
moment.
And we never will.
Shady cemetery at Flatonia, layers of Texas rest
near a major freeway where people in trucks and cars
skimming past
don’t think about any of these bones.
They don’t know
if someone worked in the cotton gin
or the creamery, if they raised chickens or goats.
Was it a house made of brick or wood?
Did she run the hotel?
We don’t know her well,
we don’t know anything.
Only Judy over at Archives could tell us
which corner of this land

holds the original Flato founders,
as we wander among
Beckhams and Wiedemanns, Agnes and Otto Olle.
What we know fits inside less than a century.
We don't like numbers much anymore.
We don't like a world that erases five or ten thousand
children who did nothing wrong to anyone,
at once, *en masse*, as if *too bad, you didn't have a chance.*
Little children of Gaza, wrapped like tight dolmade rolls in
white sheets, line the rubbled streets.
We don't like grown-ups who rationalize this,
who scurry off in protective gear
to do their next official deed.
What is happening to souls?
Are souls as hard as acorns by now?
Are they cement,
will they be granted pleasure in their future days?
Will anyone know them, and if so,
what will they say they did?

Things I Saw Before You Were Born

Car wash in ugly lot.

  Vietnamese restaurant.

Concrete bus bench fashioned to look like a tree.

I fix my eyes on them

    to remind me

who we used to be.

Swiss-styled cottage on Lullwood Street,

    once I wrote it a letter

saying I felt great joy

passing that storybook house,

they answered.

  You are welcome any time,

come over, signed *Magic House People,*

but I never did and now

it's surely too late.

I don't even know

where you live now.

Trying to remember who I was

before Mom.

Lived half my life

before being Mom.

When I make a mistake

and use your name,

your own son says,

we might as well all call each other

by his name now,

why not?

He's not using it.

Voices echoing

under sun in heat,

still waking up.

The Luxury of a Living Child

We can't even list

everything we'd do

to hang on to you.

Each day I awaken knowing

something huge can never

feel right again.

They say you're "with us always"

but it's not relatable.

I just want to make you breakfast.

Young parents go off to drive

their children, get take-out for

their children.

Letting the sun sink without

trying to hold onto it is easy.

Ten minutes of farewell feels

soothing.

But it's a stopped clock now,

our cozy lives.

Big Family

I heard of a woman
who survived her son's death
by imagining all children
as her children.
Young tattooed boys named Zack,
chubby teens with pink hair,
pigtailed girl shaping cats
from clay, sleeping babies
strapped in strollers.
And not just children either.
All the people at a crosswalk.
They're young enough to be
someone's children.
Tired families on holiday.
A neighbor walking a pup.
Men in line staring at their phones,
flexing dumb muscles.
I'm so surrounded by you now—
every Gazan baby,

every fourth-grader,
even the teenager whose car broke down
so he's walking the center
of the highway right next to
the little gray wall, so dangerous—
especially him.

That's my life now.
I have a million kids.

Spinach

Today at the last place
we ever saw you alive, I ordered
spinach, not because I like it much
but because one of us
ordered it that night and we
shared. Dipping in spoons.
Your collar crisp
even at the end of a long day,
talking felt light.

I have no idea if you still know
anything. I think of what we
might have said. Sometimes
I still say it. I tell you news.
You shake your dark head
in the top of the tree.

Today the Israelis killed 90 people
in southern Gaza hoping to kill
one guy named Muhammad.

Email

If I could just get your email address
up there beyond the stars and galaxies,
planets and floating bits of debris,
I'd tell you
everything you've missed,
how we will never be the same,
how adorable and sensitive your son is,
surely you know that,
how I wish I had never traveled to Japan or China,
anywhere that took me away from you even for a minute.
I'm so sorry,
I should have stayed glued to your side,
breathing down your neck
a little harder. If I could apologize,
how much would it be for?
Everything we didn't do that we might have.
Anything we will never understand.
If we could find a calm planet to escape to
every time we go crazy with missing you,

all our history, our private jokes
and quotes, our references,
how parents lose *all their references*
when a child dies, it might be nice.
Otherwise this feels like
no more gravity,
just bits of dust floating around
a crazy country, lost. *Cannot be delivered.*
That address, I really need it, won't abuse it,
know you probably won't answer,
you weren't very good about answering
anything ever really,
phones or letters or messages,
you were always so late,
maybe you are hearing this
and writing your reply right now,
I just won't receive it
for one hundred years.

How Are You Doing?

After your child dies,

never again *Fine*.

When people said, *You take care*,

I crumpled. What good had that done?

If innocents are slaughtered mercilessly

for years,

and the United States continues sending weapons,

Fine is no longer a word.

All people are your people,

maybe, maybe not.

The president is not my people.

The dead are my people.

After your child dies,

you feel half dead while alive,

it is hard to describe.

So you say *OK*. I guess.

Maybe OK.

Not good at all. Lost

What Ignacio Said

You must lie on your back very patiently.
Ask the ancestors to help you now,
then wait. Arms flat, stretched at your sides,
palms up. Surely the ancestors went through
similar things in even harder times.
Ask them to guide you.
Do this through your cells.
Welcome their guidance
up through hands and arms, into
body, mind and spirit.
How long will it take?
It might take a long time.
It might take forever.
I think you need to do this often.
Let them know you need them.
How did they survive?

Later

We forget what cold is like. A bus slams
into a truck at the corner, the whole
neighborhood sits up straight.
Grief, freight train in the distance
clattering on its old track.

We opened your ashes yesterday, first time.
Tried not to look at them straight on,
poured some into small bags to carry to
the islands, favorite forest, favorite beach.

And then we sealed the rest up for later.
Where is later. You will always be in it.

The Williams

Somehow the voices twined around a young mind
encouraging gentle stanzas, open endings,
even in a Texas town where they wanted you
to testify before cashing a check. Heck with that, boys.
I'm heading out in my little gray boots, slim volumes
of poetry in my holster,
William of Oregon, William of Maui,
drinking jasmine from an old fence. I'm finding a meadow,
children, dandelion puffs, scraps from a vintage notebook.
The double William of Paterson, New Jersey
helped keep us sane though our teachers
went crazy over that wheelbarrow.
Love it, then move on!
Riding a train north in England to the stoop
of another William's cottage, sloped roof,
his sister's purple-scented paper next to his,
high school memory loitering: our teacher
insisting his gloomy poem nearly led
to death. My classmates concurred,

not caring much whether some guy
leapt from a cliff long ago or not,
but I said, *He grieves, but he is filled*
with joy. In a strange voice
like a ringing bell, *immeasurable joy, because*
he grieves so much. Because he loves
so deeply all that he is seeing.
They stared at me.
I was never at home in that school.
Our teacher wanted everyone to get
the same thing from a poem.
Later home felt everywhere, radiant waters,
thistles, greenest hilltops dotted with sheep,
masses of tulips and geese, wandering William's
intricate paths, pausing at every turn,
life stretching ahead, mountains of bliss
and searing sorrow for years to come.
They wrote it, we defended it,
it seemed joyous enough to know one could
love forever, carry on or stop right there,
and the power was yours.

Where is the Wound

It is huge.

Bigger than your body.

Therefore you cannot carry it in your body.

You walk through it every day.

The gaping that greets upon awakening.

The hours before, the hours since.

They blend to suggest

they were present even before they were.

Anyone who does not apprehend the wound

is still in a state of grace.

And this you cannot hold against them.

You can admire.

Stand back.

Cup your holy hand around some air.

One June

Each calendar day

deserves to feel

as rich as the moment

an empty month turns over.

I wish we could rewind all your days

to when you were still in them.

We hold your lost hope on your birthday

and every day that you lived.

What did feeling free feel like,

free of this much sorrow?

In some ways we can never be free

while missing you.

Hold the space with us,

little squares undone.

My friend says when we give

the mind vast space,

it settles down.

Grief Blanket

"Are you and I just like specks of dust compared to the whole world?
Well you, you're bigger. You might be a spot in the carpet."
—Madison Nye, age 7

You're gray, I fold you into a rectangle

the size of a small window above a door

in an old house. Once a transom that pushed open.

We walk under you to go in or out.

Stay there. We'll find other blankets if we get cold.

We will get very cold.

After suffering for months, we know

you're bigger than we are, will remain forever close

and distant, we don't have to wonder what you're

doing every minute or try to heal.

Alone without your jokes for breeze.

It's your turn. Grieve for him. Grieve for me.

Somewhere

I need to loosen my grip

on your memory. Give it more

space

though you seem to own all space

now

oh everywhere and nowhere son.

Once you came blazing through the door

filled with rush and intention.

Hard for you to rest   those last years

which seem less like years

than a dizzying blur. I need to love

the door

more.

Though it slammed so hard.

Maybe there is still somewhere

for both of us to go.

In memory, Madison Cloudfeather Nye, 1986-2022

Acknowledgments

Grateful acknowledgement is made to the editors of the following journals in which some of these poems (or earlier versions of them) first appeared: *Beyond Bars, Columbia: A Journal for Literature & Art, Cordite Journal* (Australia), *Judith, The New York Times, Notes from the Field* (Lake Flato Architects), *One Art, Persimmon Tree, Ploughshares, Poet Lore, Presence, A Journal of Catholic Poetry, The Academy of American Poets: Poem-a-Day, The Rumpus: Poem-a-Day, Washington Square Review.*

The National Gallery of Art commissioned "'Falling Man' by Max Beckmann" in response to the painting of the same name by Max Beckmann.

"Tears, Appropriate" from *The Art of Revising Poetry,* edited by Charles Finn & Kim Stafford (Bloomsbury Publishing).

"'Those Who Knew Me Knew Me Well'" and "Where is the Wound" appeared in *The Poetry Review,* Poetry Society (London).

"Think of Me" appeared in *Improbable Worlds,* an anthology of Texas & Louisiana Poets, edited by Martha Serpas (Mutabilis Press, Houston).

"Marfa" appeared in *The Stafford Challenge Anthology, 2024-2025,* edited by Brian Rohr (Wild Poet Press).

"Driver" appeared in *Praisesong for the People* anthology, edited by Amanda Johnston (Asterism).

"Please Look Closely" appeared in *Letters to Palestine: Writers Respond to War and Occupation,* edited by Vijay Prashad (Verso Books).

"The Williams" appeared in *Invisible Strings, 113 Poets Respond to the Songs of Taylor Swift,* edited by Kristie Frederick Daugherty (Ballantine Books).

"Red Legs" appeared in *Birdbrains: A Lyrical Guide to Washington State Birds,* edited by Rich/Delaney/Seki (Raven Chronicles).

I am very grateful to Michael Nye, Marion Winik, Peter Conners & everyone at Boa Editions (our 6th book together!), Daniel Anastasio & the Agarita musicians, Texas State University Creative Writing students, R & R Collective, The Academy of American Poets, The Poetry Foundation, The Texas Institute of Letters, Texas Commission on the Arts, Humanities Texas, and all our beautiful encouraging friends.

About the Author

Palestinian-American writer, editor and educator Naomi Shihab Nye grew up in St. Louis, Jerusalem, and San Antonio, Texas, where she graduated from Trinity University and continues to live. On past faculty at Texas State University and the Michener Center for Writers, she has been Young People's Poet Laureate for the U.S. (Poetry Foundation), poetry editor for *The New York Times Magazine* and *The Texas Observer,* and a visiting writer in hundreds of schools and communities all over the world. Her books include *Grace Notes* (Poems About Families), *Everything Comes Next, The Tiny Journalist, Voices in the Air, Sitti's Secrets, Habibi, This Same Sky,* & *The Tree is Older than You Are: Poems & Paintings from Mexico.* Her volume *19 Varieties of Gazelle: Poems of the Middle East,* was a finalist for the National Book Award. *The Turtle of Oman* and *The Turtle of Michigan* have both been part of the Little Read program, North Carolina. She has received the Wallace Stevens Award from the Academy of American Poets, the Texas Writer Award 2024, and Lifetime Achievement Awards from The Texas Institute of Letters, the Arab American National Museum, and the National Book Critics Circle.

Boa Editions American Poets Continuum Series

No. 1 *The Fuhrer Bunker: A Cycle of Poems in Progress*
W. D. Snodgrass

No. 2 *She*
M. L. Rosenthal

No. 3 *Living With Distance*
Ralph J. Mills, Jr.

No. 4 *Not Just Any Death*
Michael Waters

No. 5 *That Was Then: New and Selected Poems*
Isabella Gardner

No. 6 *Things That Happen Where There Aren't Any People*
William Stafford

No. 7 *The Bridge of Change: Poems 1974–1980*
John Logan

No. 8 *Signatures*
Joseph Stroud

No. 9 *People Live Here: Selected Poems 1949–1983*
Louis Simpson

No. 10 *Yin*
Carolyn Kizer

No. 11 *Duhamel: Ideas of Order in Little Canada*
Bill Tremblay

No. 12 *Seeing It Was So*
Anthony Piccione

No. 13 *Hyam Plutzik: The Collected Poems*

No. 14 *Good Woman: Poems and a Memoir 1969–1980*
Lucille Clifton

No. 15 *Next: New Poems*
Lucille Clifton

No. 16 *Roxa: Voices of the Culver Family*
William B. Patrick

No. 17 *John Logan: The Collected Poems*

No. 18 *Isabella Gardner: The Collected Poems*

No. 19 *The Sunken Lightship*
Peter Makuck

No. 20 *The City in Which I Love You*
Li-Young Lee

No. 21 *Quilting: Poems 1987–1990*
Lucille Clifton

No. 22 *John Logan: The Collected Fiction*

No. 23 *Shenandoah and Other Verse Plays*
Delmore Schwartz

No. 24 *Nobody Lives on Arthur Godfrey Boulevard*
Gerald Costanzo

No. 25 *The Book of Names: New and Selected Poems*
Barton Sutter

No. 26 *Each in His Season*
W. D. Snodgrass

No. 27 *Wordworks: Poems Selected and New*
Richard Kostelanetz

No. 28 *What We Carry*
Dorianne Laux

No. 29 *Red Suitcase*
Naomi Shihab Nye

No. 30 *Song*
Brigit Pegeen Kelly

No. 31 *The Fuehrer Bunker: The Complete Cycle*
W. D. Snodgrass

No. 32 *For the Kingdom*
Anthony Piccione

No. 33 *The Quicken Tree*
Bill Knott

No. 34 *These Upraised Hands*
William B. Patrick

No. 35 *Crazy Horse in Stillness*
William Heyen

No. 36 *Quick, Now, Always*
Mark Irwin

No. 37 *I Have Tasted the Apple*
Mary Crow

No. 38 *The Terrible Stories*
Lucille Clifton

No. 39 *The Heat of Arrivals*
Ray Gonzalez

No. 40 *Jimmy & Rita*
Kim Addonizio

No. 41 *Green Ash, Red Maple, Black Gum*
Michael Waters

No. 42 *Against Distance*
Peter Makuck

No. 43 *The Night Path*
Laurie Kutchins

No. 44 *Radiography*
Bruce Bond

No. 45 *At My Ease: Uncollected Poems of the Fifties and Sixties*
David Ignatow

No. 46 *Trillium*
Richard Foerster

No. 47 *Fuel*
Naomi Shihab Nye

No. 48 *Gratitude*
Sam Hamill

No. 49 *Diana, Charles, & the Queen*
William Heyen

No. 50 *Plus Shipping*
Bob Hicok

No. 51 *Cabato Sentora*
Ray Gonzalez

No. 52 *We Didn't Come Here for This*
William B. Patrick

No. 53 *The Vandals*
Alan Michael Parker

No. 54 *To Get Here*
Wendy Mnookin

No. 55 *Living Is What I Wanted: Last Poems*
David Ignatow

No. 56 *Dusty Angel*
Michael Blumenthal

No. 57 *The Tiger Iris*
Joan Swift

No. 58 *White City*
Mark Irwin

No. 59 *Laugh at the End of the World: Collected Comic Poems 1969–1999*
Bill Knott

No. 60 *Blessing the Boats: New and Selected Poems: 1988–2000*
Lucille Clifton

No. 61 *Tell Me*
Kim Addonizio

No. 62 *Smoke*
Dorianne Laux

No. 63 *Parthenopi: New and Selected Poems*
Michael Waters

No. 64 *Rancho Notorious*
Richard Garcia

No. 65 *Jam*
Joe-Anne McLaughlin

No. 66 *A. Poulin, Jr. Selected Poems*
Edited, with an Introduction by Michael Waters

No. 67 *Small Gods of Grief*
Laure-Anne Bosselaar

No. 68 *Book of My Nights*
Li-Young Lee

No. 69 *Tulip Farms and Leper Colonies*
Charles Harper Webb

No. 70 *Double Going*
Richard Foerster

No. 71 *What He Took*
Wendy Mnookin

No. 72 *The Hawk Temple at Tierra Grande*
Ray Gonzalez

No. 73 *Mules of Love*
Ellen Bass

No. 74 *The Guests at the Gate*
Anthony Piccione

No. 75 *Dumb Luck*
Sam Hamill

No. 76 *Love Song with Motor Vehicles*
Alan Michael Parker

No. 77 *Life Watch*
Willis Barnstone

No. 78 *The Owner of the House: New Collected Poems 1940–2001*
Louis Simpson

No. 79 *Is*
Wayne Dodd

No. 80 *Late*
Cecilia Woloch

No. 81 *Precipitates*
Debra Kang Dean

No. 82 *The Orchard*
Brigit Pegeen Kelly

No. 83 *Bright Hunger*
Mark Irwin

No. 84 *Desire Lines: New and Selected Poems*
Lola Haskins

No. 85 *Curious Conduct*
Jeanne Marie Beaumont

No. 86 *Mercy*
Lucille Clifton

No. 87 *Model Homes*
Wayne Koestenbaum

No. 88 *Farewell to the Starlight in Whiskey*
Barton Sutter

No. 89 *Angels for the Burning*
David Mura

No. 90 *The Rooster's Wife*
Russell Edson

No. 91 *American Children*
Jim Simmerman

No. 92 *Postcards from the Interior*
Wyn Cooper

No. 93 *You & Yours*
Naomi Shihab Nye

No. 94 *Consideration of the Guitar: New and Selected Poems 1986–2005*
Ray Gonzalez

No. 95 *Off-Season in the Promised Land*
Peter Makuck

No. 96 *The Hoopoe's Crown*
Jacqueline Osherow

No. 97 *Not for Specialists: New and Selected Poems*
W. D. Snodgrass

No. 98 *Splendor*
Steve Kronen

No. 99 *Woman Crossing a Field*
Deena Linett

No. 134 *The Collected Poems of Lucille Clifton: 1965–2010*

No. 135 *To Keep Love Blurry*
Craig Morgan Teicher

No. 136 *Theophobia*
Bruce Beasley

No. 137 *Refuge*
Adrie Kusserow

No. 138 *The Book of Goodbyes*
Jillian Weise

No. 139 *Birth Marks*
Jim Daniels

No. 140 *No Need of Sympathy*
Fleda Brown

No. 141 *There's a Box in the Garage You Can Beat with a Stick*
Michael Teig

No. 142 *The Keys to the Jail*
Keetje Kuipers

No. 143 *All You Ask for Is Longing: New and Selected Poems 1994–2014*
Sean Thomas Dougherty

No. 144 *Copia*
Erika Meitner

No. 145 *The Chair: Prose Poems*
Richard Garcia

No. 146 *In a Landscape*
John Gallaher

No. 147 *Fanny Says*
Nickole Brown

No. 148 *Why God Is a Woman*
Nin Andrews

No. 149 *Testament*
G.C. Waldrep

No. 150 *I'm No Longer Troubled by the Extravagance*
Rick Bursky

No. 151 *Antidote for Night*
Marsha de la O

No. 152 *Beautiful Wall*
Ray Gonzalez

No. 153 *the black maria*
Aracelis Girmay

No. 154 *Celestial Joyride*
Michael Waters

No. 155 *Whereso*
Karen Volkman

No. 156 *The Day's Last Light Reddens the Leaves of the Copper Beech*
Stephen Dobyns

No. 157 *The End of Pink*
Kathryn Nuernberger

No. 158 *Mandatory Evacuation*
Peter Makuck

No. 159 *Primitive: The Art and Life of Horace H. Pippin*
Janice N. Harrington

No. 160 *The Trembling Answers*
Craig Morgan Teicher

No. 161 *Bye-Bye Land*
Christian Barter

No. 162 *Sky Country*
Christine Kitano

No. 163 *All Soul Parts Returned*
Bruce Beasley

No. 164 *The Smoke of Horses*
Charles Rafferty

No. 165 *The Second O of Sorrow*
Sean Thomas Dougherty

No. 166 *Holy Moly Carry Me*
Erika Meitner

No. 167 *Clues from the Animal Kingdom*
Christopher Kennedy

No. 168 *Dresses from the Old Country*
Laura Read

No. 169 *In Country*
Hugh Martin

No. 170 *The Tiny Journalist*
Naomi Shihab Nye

No. 171 *All Its Charms*
Keetje Kuipers

No. 172 *Night Angler*
Geffrey Davis

No. 173 *The Human Half*
Deborah Brown

No. 174 *Cyborg Detective*
Jillian Weise

No. 175 *On the Shores of Welcome Home*
Bruce Weigl

No. 176 *Rue*
Kathryn Nuernberger

No. 177 *Let's Become a Ghost Story*
Rick Bursky

No. 178 *Year of the Dog*
Deborah Paredez

No. 179 *Brand New Spacesuit*
John Gallaher

No. 180 *How to Carry Water: Selected Poems of Lucille Clifton*
Edited, with an Introduction by Aracelis Girmay

No. 181 *Caw*
Michael Waters

No. 182 *Letters to a Young Brown Girl*
Barbara Jane Reyes

No. 183 *Mother Country*
Elana Bell

No. 184 *Welcome to Sonnetville, New Jersey*
Craig Morgan Teicher

No. 185 *I Am Not Trying to Hide My Hungers from the World*
Kendra DeColo

No. 186 *The Naomi Letters*
Rachel Mennies

No. 187 *Tenderness*
Derrick Austin

No. 188 *Ceive*
B.K. Fischer

No. 189 *Diamonds*
Camille Guthrie

No. 190 *A Cluster of Noisy Planets*
Charles Rafferty

No. 191 *Useful Junk*
Erika Meitner

No. 192 *Field Notes from the Flood Zone*
Heather Sellers

No. 193 *A Season in Hell with Rimbaud*
Dustin Pearson

No. 194 *Your Emergency Contact Has Experienced an Emergency*
Chen Chen

No. 195 *A Tinderbox in Three Acts*
Cynthia Dewi Oka

No. 196 *Little Mr. Prose Poem: Selected Poems of Russell Edson*
Edited by Craig Morgan Teicher

No. 197 *The Dug-Up Gun Museum*
Matt Donovan

No. 198 *Four in Hand*
Alicia Mountain

No. 199 *Buffalo Girl*
Jessica Q. Stark

No. 200 *Nomenclatures of Invisibility*
Mahtem Shiferraw

No. 201 *Flare, Corona*
Jeannine Hall Gailey

No. 202 *Death Prefers the Minor Keys*
Sean Thomas Dougherty

No. 203 *Desire Museum*
Danielle Deulen

No. 204 *Transitory*
Subhaga Crystal Bacon
No. 205 *Every Hard Sweetness*
Sheila Carter-Jones
No. 206 *Blue on a Blue Palette*
Lynne Thompson
No. 207 *One Wild Word Away*
Geffrey Davis
No. 208 *The Strange God Who Makes Us*
Christopher Kennedy
No. 209 *Our Splendid Failure to Do the Impossible*
Rebecca Lindenberg
No. 210 *Yard Show*
Janice N. Harrington
No. 211 *The Last Song of the World*
Joseph Fasano
No. 212 *Lonely Women Make Good Lovers*
Keetje Kuipers
No. 213 *jump the gun*
Jennie Malboeuf
No. 214 *Apostle of Desire*
Bruce Weigl
No. 215 *GREEN OF ALL HEADS*
Aracelis Girmay
No. 216 *Pluck*
Adam Hughes
No. 217 *Disaster Tourism*
Rena J. Mosteirin
No. 218 *The Appendectomy Grin*
Charles Rafferty
No. 219 *The Serious World*
Laura Read
No. 220 *At the Gate: Uncollected Poems 1987–2010*
Lucille Clifton
Edited by Kazim Ali
No. 221 *August, September, October*
Craig Morgan Teicher
No. 222 *This Elegance*
Derrick Austin
No. 223 *Sidekick*
Naomi Shihab Nye

Colophon

Boa Editions, a nonprofit publisher of poetry and other literary works, fosters readership and appreciation of contemporary literature. By identifying, cultivating, and publishing both new and established poets and selecting authors of unique literary talent, Boa brings high-quality literature to the public.

Support for this effort comes from the sale of its publications, grant funding, and private donations.

The publication of this book is made possible, in part, by the special support of the following individuals:

Anonymous (x2)

Amy Betti, *In memory of Rachel Corrie*

Angela Bonazinga & Catherine Lewis

Caccamise Foundation

Bernadette Catalana

Christopher Dahl

Bonnie Garner

Robert Giron

Albert Goldbarth

Alison Granucci

Janice N. Harrington & Robert Parker

Peg Heminway

Grant Holcomb

Nora A. Jones

Kitty & Nick Jospe

Joe & Dale Klein

Hugh Martin

Daniel M. Meyers, *In honor of J. Shepard Skiff*

Joe McElveney

Boo Poulin, *In memory of A. Poulin, Jr.*

Matthew Shenoda

Meredith & Adam Smith

Deborah Ronnen

David W. Ryon

William Waddell & Linda Rubel

"Raise Your Voice" Capital Campaign Supporters

In honor of Boa's 50th anniversary, the following individuals made significant contributions to our "Raise Your Voice" Capital Campaign. We are grateful for their generous support. To learn how to join the chorus and raise your voice to ensure another 50 years of independent publishing visit: www.boaeditions.org.

Anonymous

Kathleen Holcombe

Joe & Dale Klein

William Waddell & Linda Rubel